The Word Of God

Awaken A Passion For The Bible

Micah Level

The Word Of God by Micah level

lovepursuitinternational.com

Cover design and layout by Micah Level.

Scripture quotations are from The ESV® Bible (The Holy Bible, English Standard Version®), copyright © 2001 by Crossway, a publishing ministry of Good News Publishers. Used by permission. All rights reserved.

This book or parts thereof may not be reproduced in any form, stored in a retrieval system, or transmitted in any form by any means—electronic, mechanical, photocopy, recording, or otherwise—without prior written permission of the author, except as provided by United States of America copyright law.

Copyright © 2020 Micah Level

All rights reserved.

ISBN: 9798632559997

Contents

Opening

God desires to stir up in us a hunger and faith for the Word. How we perceive the Bible is how we will approach the Bible. If we perceive it as a history book or an instruction manual then that is the way we will treat and value it. We all have manuals in our homes for our appliances and electronics, but they stay on a shelf and collect dust until we really need them. If a crisis arises and one of our appliances breaks down, we go to it for instruction. In the same way, if we see the Bible only as a manual we will approach it that way. We'll only run to it in the midst of a life crisis. If we perceive it for what it truly is, the very Word of God, then we will approach it for daily life. God's desire is to impart and deposit in us a love and passion for the Bible. His very Word.

"Man shall not live by bread alone, but by every word that comes from the mouth of God." Matthew 4:4

We need the Word of God, not for moments of crisis but for daily living. Culture has drifted so far from the truth and standard of His Word. If we as His people aren't staying in it, then who will? If we're not living from the Word of the Father, then who will live from the Word of the Father?

"faith comes from hearing, and hearing through the word of Christ." Romans 10:17

Faith comes from hearing. Our ability to hear comes from the Word of Christ.

His Word opens our ears to hear His voice! When we stay in His Word our ears stay attuned and open to His living voice. When we hear, faith comes! Faith is solely; the product of hearing His Word. It doesn't come from our own mind or conclusions, it comes from His Word! The Bible is our hearing aid to the voice of God.

In this moment of time God is going to unlock and release fresh revelation to us. This coming revelation will be from the Word of God. The Lord is calling us back to the Bible! There is still untapped revelation inside His Word. If the Word were a maple tree, we haven't even come close to tapping out all the syrup and nutrients from it. We will never reach the bottom of it. Even with two thousand years of revelation passed down in the church, we still haven't even scratched the surface. We don't even know Scriptures that we think we know. Revelation that has been unnoticed and untapped in the Word will be revealed to us in this day and age. Scriptures that have been read over and over will be seen in a new light.

The revelation that is coming will be from the integrity of the complete and undivided nature of the Word of God, but will be multifaceted in meaning.

In the church, we can find people who have multifaceted revelation from spiritual experiences, but who lose the love and passion for the integrity of the Bible. They run from encounter to encounter and revelation to revelation, casting off the belt of truth. This is dangerous. What God is releasing today is spiritual revelation that will be multifaceted, having many meanings and interpretations, but will be rooted and founded upon the integrity of the Bible.

The Word of God is twofold in nature and both expressed by the living Spirit: Logos and Rhema. Logos is the thoughts and revelations of God. Rhema is the speaking of God. First come the thoughts and revelation of God then come the speaking. The living voice of the Spirit unlocks the logos (thoughts and revelation of God) and releases rhema (speaks) to our spirit.

The Word contains the revelation of God's nature and character. We can discover a lot about a person by what comes out of their mouth.

"The good person out of the good treasure of his heart produces good, and the evil person out of his evil treasure produces evil, for out of the abundance of the heart his mouth speaks." Luke 6:45

Out of the abundance of the heart (the nature and character of the person) the mouth speaks! Words are formed from the overflow of the heart. Words reveal the character of a person. The Bible is the Word of God! It reveals His character to us. The Word reveals the author to us. We read the Word of God to know the God of the Word. It's so important to stay rooted in the Word, because the Word reveals to us His grand plan and purpose.

The Word Of God: Awaken A Passion For The Bible is written to stir up a hunger for the Word inside of you. The Lord is going to awaken a new passion for the Bible in your life. The Word is going to come alive to you and in you. You will join the psalmist and say, "I rejoice at your word like one who finds great spoil." Psalms 119:162

The Bible Is Breathed Out By God

To have a proper foundation of faith for the Bible, we must see it and approach it for what it truly is: the very Word of God! It has been breathed out by His mouth.

"Indeed, all who desire to live a godly life in Christ Jesus will be persecuted, while evil people and impostors will go on from bad to worse, deceiving and being deceived. But as for you, continue in what you have learned and have firmly believed, knowing from whom you learned it and how from childhood you have been acquainted with the sacred writings, which are able to make you wise for salvation through faith in Christ Jesus. All Scripture is breathed out by God and profitable for teaching, for reproof, for correction, and for training in righteousness, that the man of God may be complete, equipped for every good work." 2 Timothy 3:12-17

We are encouraged to avoid going from bad to worse and deceiving to being deceived. How do we do that? We continue in the Bible. We come to it as the breathed out Word of God! It is His Word, written on paper. It was inspired by the very breath of God and scribed by man. It was authored by God Himself. Moses wasn't an author, he was a scribe. Paul wasn't an author, he was a scribe.

"We have the prophetic word more fully confirmed, to which you will do well to pay attention as to a lamp shining in a dark place, until the day dawns and the morning star rises in your hearts, knowing this first of all, that no prophecy of Scripture comes from someone's own interpretation. For no prophecy was ever produced by the will of man, but men spoke from God as they were carried along by the Holy Spirit." 2 Peter 1:19-21

Men spoke from God as they were carried along by the Holy Spirit. Every one of them was a scribe for the mouth of God. The same Voice that spoke the universe into existence and breathed life into Adam, spoke the Word inside the Bible.

Many books are profitable for entertainment, learning, and filling the mind with knowledge, but only the Bible is profitable for teaching, reproof, correction, and training in righteousness. Only His Word will complete us and equip us for every good work. Every book in the universe speaks to our mind, but only the Bible speaks to our spirit. His Word speaks Spirit to spirit! God's Spirit to our spirit.

The Word Created All Things

"By the word of the Lord the heavens were made, and by the breath of his mouth all their host." Psalms 33:6

Everything was created by the very Word of the Lord. The same mouth that created all things created the Bible.

"By faith we understand that the universe was created by the word of God, so that what is seen was not made out of things that are visible." Hebrews 11:3

The entire universe was created by the Word of God. If the Word created the universe what can it create in us? The Word is so valuable. It is the most valuable thing in the World.

"He is the radiance of the glory of God and the exact imprint of his nature, and he upholds the universe by the word of his power. After making purification for sins, he sat down at the right hand of the Majesty on high," Hebrews 1:3

The entire universe is upheld by the Word of His power. When we open the Bible we aren't just reading advice or instructions. We read the very Word that holds us together. The Voice that sustains us speaks in every page and verse.

The Word Is Eternal

In the beginning was the Word and the Word was with God, and the Word was God. He was in the beginning with God. All things were made through him, and without him was not any thing made that was made." John 1:1-3

The Word was in the beginning. It has been since before libraries, and the internet. All these things are gifts for our benefit, but they aren't the Word of God. Videos, books, and blogs come and go, but the Word is eternal and remains. The Word has been since before all things, but too often we can be found running to everything under the sun except for the Word of God. When we feed on everything but the Word we lose our effectiveness in society. We lose our salt and light in culture. We were created to be a pillar of the truth in our world. Politics and pop culture aren't the solution for today's problems, the Word is! The Word carries solutions into every PRESENT problem.

"The grass withers, the flower fades, but the word of our God will stand forever." Isaiah 40:8

Everything fades. Our own words fade. His eternal Word stands forever.

"Simon Peter answered him, "Lord, to whom shall we go? You have the words of eternal life," John 6:68

Can you think of a book on the earth that has eternal words? There is no other than the Bible. Jesus alone has Words of eternal life. His Word drips life and releases life to the hearer because it is eternal.

"Since you have been born again, not of perishable seed but of imperishable, through the living and abiding word of God;" 1 Peter 1:23

The Word of God is one: living and two: abiding. It holds the life of God and it endures like Him throughout time.

The Word is Spirit

"It is the Spirit who gives life; the flesh is no help at all. The words that I have spoken to you are spirit and life." John 6:63

The Word is Spirit and life. Do we come to the Bible in faith that it is the very Word of God? Or is it just a history book and manual with dry words? Do we come with a faith that the Word is spirit and life? That it is supernatural in nature? The Word releases spiritual strength to our spirit man! It brings life to our physical man.

The Word is Spirit, meaning it exists outside of this dimension. We are confined to the three dimensions of space and the one dimension of time, but the Word isn't constrained to that! It exists outside of the realms of time and space. His Word is supernatural. It supersedes the natural realm. It exists in the Spirit Realm. That realm has multiple dimensions. His Word can weave in and out of our dimension of time and space. The same Word that spoke to Abraham, Moses, and King David is here presently speaking to you and me.

"For who knows a person's thoughts except the spirit of that person, which is in him? So also no one comprehends the thoughts of God except the Spirit of God. Now we have received not the spirit of the world, but the Spirit who is from God, that we might understand the things freely given us by God. And we impart this in words not taught by human wisdom but taught by the Spirit, interpreting spiritual truths to those who are spiritual." 1 Corinthians 2:11-13

We only know the thoughts of God by the Spirit. The Word is not human wisdom, but spiritual truth. The Word supersedes nature. It created this realm. Which is more powerful? This created physical realm, or the Spirit Word that created it? The answer is the Word.

"He sent out his word and healed them, and delivered them from their destruction." Psalms 107:20

He didn't send out His power or His life! He sent out His Word. Why? Because His Word is spirit and life! His Word can create and alter this dimension of time and space. It has the power to eradicate sickness and death in the body! The Word exists in the Spirit dimension and influences this physical dimension. The Word is not natural words meant for the mind, they are Spirit words meant for our spirit.

The Word Is A Mirror

"Anyone who listens to the word but does not do what it says is like someone who looks at his face in a mirror and, after looking at himself, goes away and immediately forgets what he looks like." James 1:22-25

The Word of God is a mirror that reflects the image and identity of God. When we read it we discover who He is and who we are. We can trust and believe everything it says about the image of God and our identity in Him. We can put all our confidence in it because it is a mirror! We simply trust the mirror. No one would try to discover what they look like by turning their skin inside out. That would be silly! All we need is a mirror to figure out what we look like. A mirror is the only way that we know and can confidently tell others our hair and eye color. Our identity is not self-made. It only comes from the Word. Our identity is found in Christ's image. We are called to be image bearers. In the Word we look on the image of Christ and take on His likeness. As we look intently into the mirror of the Word we will discover the image and identity of God, and in turn our personal identity and image will align to it. Rather than adjusting the Word to line up with our own life, our life is adjusted to line up with the Word. All our thoughts and intentions are exposed. Every area of our life and thinking that is not aligned to the image in the Word is challenged and confronted. As we daily behold the Lord in the mirror our life is transformed and renewed!

The Word Feeds Us

"Man shall not live by bread alone, but by every word that comes from the mouth of God." Matthew 4:4

How do we live physically? We must eat and drink. But the Word is a greater food! Food and drink is confined to this realm, but the Word is food from a different realm. Humanity wines, dines, and dies, but those who eat and drink the Word, find life!

"For the word of God is living and active, sharper than any two-edged sword, piercing to the division of soul and of spirit, of joints and of marrow, and discerning the thoughts and intentions of the heart." Hebrews 4:12

The Word is living and active! It isn't dead and stagnant. Have you found that no matter what season you are in, you can turn to the Bible and find something that applies to you? How is it that millions read the Word and find encouragement and strength for their unique situation? Because it is living and active. It isn't a history lesson or a nice guide and instruction manual. It is the very living Word of God. It actively engages our spirit and speaks to us!

The Word cuts and divides our life to line up with the Word. Our life and beliefs aren't formed by our circumstances or what the world tells us, but by the word of God in our heart. If we want to be like the world, then let our thinking be dictated by the words of the world. If you want to be like Jesus, then let our life be dictated by the Word of God.

We must be fed from the Word of a different realm. We can't be formed by this dimension, we must be formed by His. The Word says if we walk by the Spirit we will not gratify the desires of the flesh. If we only feed ourselves with flesh words we will get flesh works. If we feed ourselves with Spirit Words we will get spirit fruits.

The Word Transforms Us

"Do not be conformed to this world, but be transformed by the renewal of your mind, that by testing you may discern what is the will of God, what is good and acceptable and perfect." Romans 12:2

We aren't called to be conformed to this world. We are called to be transformed by the Word. The world and the things of the world are the lust of the eyes, the hunger for power, riches, and fame. It's a whole system and way of doing things. It is the work of immorality. We aren't called to conform to this pattern. God has always intended for us to be counter culture. We are called to be an opposing stream to the current of the World, transformed by the Word.

The spirit of the world entices us. It wants us to conform, to follow the course of the world, to walk in similar form and type. The spirit of the world is governed by a lust for power, money, and fame. It wants to be powerful and control with fear. It is dictated by money, and to seek self exaltation. It is the works of the flesh.

We are in the world, but not of the world. We live in this system but we do things differently. We have a different culture, a different pattern. If we aren't in the Word we will find ourselves conforming to the pattern of this world, seeking after power, wealth, and fame. Sadly, if we look at a lot of the present ministers out there, we would think that success with God was having thousands of followers on social media and thousands of YouTube subscribers. We can begin to think that if we were a radical Christian or church we would be famous. This is the pattern of the world. God wants to bless us and give us influence to be impactful for His Gospel. This isn't money, power, and fame. We aren't called to chase these things. That is earthly and demonic.

We aren't called to look like the world. We are called to look like the Word. The world works to conform us. God's word transforms us! Conform means to be similar in form or type, to comply with culture. This isn't how we are to live: going to heaven, but living like hell, hearing His Word, but living like the World. The conformity of the world puts us to sleep. It sings a demonic lullaby. We aren't called to be a sleeping beauty. We must be awake! Jesus will return and He's not coming for a sleeping church. He is coming for an awakened bride. We must be awake in His Word, not sleeping in the world.

Transform means to make a thorough or dramatic change in the form, appearance, or character. God wants to transform us! His Word makes a dramatic change in our form, appearance, and character. When we feast on the Word we put on the Word!
The Word feeds us a different pattern to be formed by: the pattern of God, and the image of Christ. The Word says the greatest will

serve. It says do not worry about money, but seek His kingdom. It says do nothing from selfish ambition or conceit, but in humility count others more significant than yourselves. The Word became flesh in Jesus and God's goal is for His Word to become flesh in you and me. As we remain in it, we take on His form and appearance. We become living epistles for the world to read. Our marriages are different, our character is different, our words are different, our homes are different, the way we look at money is different, and the way we lead is different. Everything about us is different.

We are called to "be blameless and innocent, children of God without blemish in the midst of a crooked and twisted generation, among whom you shine as lights in the world, holding fast to the word of life." Philippians 2:15-16

We are called to be awake in the midst of this crooked and twisted generation. We are called to be in the world and love the world, but we aren't called to look like the world or be friends with it. We've come so close to it that we've allowed ourselves to be conformed to it. We are called to love this generation, but until this generation comes into Christ they are crooked and twisted. The wisdom of this world is demonic. God's Word imparts spiritual wisdom. We've grown infatuated with the world, we must grow in love with the Word, because if we aren't living from the Spirit of the Word we will be led by the spirit of the World.

"Know this, my beloved brothers: let every person be quick to hear, slow to speak, slow to anger; for the anger of man does not produce the righteousness of God. Therefore put away all filthiness and rampant wickedness and receive with meekness the implanted word, which is able to save your souls." James 1:19-21

The implanted Word saves our soul. It works in us our salvation and righteousness: Christ! It transforms us into His image.

We may be inspired and motivated by experiences, demonstrations, and manifestations, but it is only the Word that has the power to truly transform our souls. We must not build on experience, we must build on the Word.

The Word Cleans Us

"Husbands, love your wives, as Christ loved the church and gave himself up for her, that he might sanctify her, having cleansed her by the washing of water with the word, so that he might present the church to himself in splendor, without spot or wrinkle or any such thing, that she might be holy and without blemish." Ephesians 5:25-27

How will we be presented to Christ in splendor, without spot or wrinkle, holy and without blemish? By the washing water of the Word! As we remain in the Word we discover the righteousness of Christ and are daily cleansed and washed by it.

When Jesus washed the disciples' feet Peter wanted to be washed all over, but Jesus told him "The one who has bathed does not need to wash, except for his feet, but is completely clean. And you are clean." John 13:10. They were already washed and clean, but their feet got dirty from walking in the world. In the same way, we who are in Christ are already washed. We have been baptized in the water and the blood. We have been cleansed from all unrighteousness. The waters of baptism have washed away our unclean and dirty man. We have risen to new life in Christ. We have been made pure in His eyes. We have also been covered by His blood. His blood has cleaned us and washed us, but we live in a dirty and dusty world. As we walk in this broken world as ambassadors of Christ, our feet get a little dirty, so we come to the Word and find daily washing for our feet.

"Already you are clean because of the word that I have spoken to you." John 15:3

His Word is what cleans and washes. This is supernatural! No other words have the ability to wash and clean us. The Bible isn't just words on a piece of paper. It isn't human words of wisdom. It is the Word of God. Through the Holy Spirit, the expressed thoughts of God become the voice of God, and as we approach it we are washed and refreshed! The Word infuses us, it cleans us, and it regenerates us.

The Word Gives Wisdom

"For the Lord gives wisdom; from his mouth come knowledge and understanding;" Proverbs 2:6

The Lord is the one who releases wisdom! His mouth (Word) brings it forth. We discover His will and wisdom by remaining in His Word.

"Let the word of Christ dwell in you richly, teaching and admonishing one another in all wisdom, singing psalms and hymns and spiritual songs, with thankfulness in your hearts to God." Colossians 3:16

When we let the Word of Christ dwell in us richly, we teach and admonish one another in ALL wisdom. As the thoughts and revelation of God abundantly take up residence in the realm inside of us, we teach and admonish one another in wisdom. The Word gives us sharp vision and keen observation for our time. We are clothed in the wisdom from above.

Abide In His Word

"If you abide in me, and my words abide in you, ask whatever you wish, and it will be done for you." John 15:7

The basis for answered prayer is abiding in His Word. God doesn't work beyond His Word. Desperate prayers or spiritual gimmicks do not work. "If you sow this, you will reap this! If you pray this way, you will see results." No! Only the Word. The Word in your mouth has the same power as the Word in God's mouth. He honors His Word.

"So Jesus said to the Jews who had believed him, "If you abide in my word, you are truly my disciples, and you will know the truth, and the truth will set you free."" John 8:31-32

When we abide in His Word, we are truly His disciples. The solution to learning and growing in discipleship is the Word. We have made being a disciple complicated. It is simple: remain in His Word. We will know the truth and it will set us free! It will transform us! It's impossible to remain lukewarm when we feast on the Word. We can feed on other people's words and remain lukewarm. How do we become a disciple? Get in the Word!

""Everyone then who hears these words of mine and does them will be like a wise man who built his house on the rock. And the rain fell, and the floods came, and the winds blew and beat on that house, but it did not fall, because it had been founded on the rock. And everyone who hears these words of mine and does not do them will be like a foolish man who built his house on the sand. And the rain fell, and the floods came, and the winds blew and beat against that house, and it fell, and great was the fall of it.""
Matthew 7:24-27

As we abide in His Word (hearing and doing it) our life is built on the rock (Christ) and no storm or circumstance will be able to make us fall.

Closing

I remember when I was an 8 month old new believer, I suddenly found myself struggling in my faith and emotions. Old temptations and habits were knocking at my door. I was experiencing an intense demonic attack of lies. One night, in the midst of all this, I came to my dad crying and said "Dad I don't know what to do! I am having all these crazy thoughts. I can't sleep! I feel sad. I have doubts!" I was in a state of battle and confusion. My dad looked me in the eye and said, "Micah, take the word like medicine! It may not taste good to you initially. You may struggle to read it. But like medicine, even if it tastes bad, you take it knowing it will make you healthy. It will make you well."

That moment changed my life. I will never forget that statement and what it did in me. I suddenly knew I could take the Word of God like medicine for my soul. That very day I began to apply my dad's prescription. I dove into my Bible and soon enough, the lies went quiet, the negative feelings left, and the doubts dissolved. I discovered that the Bible truly is the Word of God. It feeds me. It gives me wisdom. It transforms me. It is more than a manual or an instruction book. It holds the very Words of Life, the very Voice of God.

"Blessed is the man who walks not in the counsel of the wicked, nor stands in the way of sinners, nor sits in the seat of scoffers; but his delight is in the law of the Lord, and on his law he meditates day and night. He is like a tree planted by streams of water that yields its fruit in its season, and its leaf does not wither. In all that he does, he prospers."
Psalms 1:1-3 ESV

We are blessed when we avoid the counsel of the wicked and choose to delight in

His Word. Rather than feeding on the media, Facebook or Youtube, or whatever else the world says, we can feed our life on the WORD of God. Our first response in the midst of "issues" or "success" is often to talk with all our friends about it or post about it on social media. This passage is essentially saying instead of getting counsel from the world, get council from the Word. Delight in His Word and instructions. At every moment and season we have the greatest gift available to us: the Bible, the book that holds the very Word of God. As we daily meditate on His Word we become like a tree planted by streams of water that yields its fruit in its season, its leaf does not wither, and in all that we do we prosper.

Today the Lord is calling us to His Word. He is imparting and depositing a love and passion for the Bible inside us. Revelation that has been unnoticed and untapped in the Word will be revealed to us. Scriptures that have been read over and over will be seen in a new light. God is releasing a spirit of wisdom and revelation to see the integrity and multifacets of His precious Word!

Closing Prayer:

God, I thank you for Your Word. I value and cherish It. I ask you to awaken a new passion and love for the Bible inside of me. Create in me a hunger for your Word. Let the Word come alive to me! Give me fresh eyes to see and ears to hear Your Word. Make me a person of Your Word, that I would abide in it and feed upon it and that it would dwell in me richly. Thank you for your empowering grace! I receive and say Amen!

Four Practical Tips

"devote yourself to the public reading of Scripture, to exhortation, to teaching." 1 Timothy 4:13

"I will meditate on your precepts and fix my eyes on your ways. I will delight in your statutes; I will not forget your word." Psalms 119:15-16

One: Savor the Word. This is meditation. We don't have to read it like a book. Instead of feeling like you have to read a whole book in a sitting, spend time meditating on one verse. Chew on one verse. I have often spent 6 months to a year meditating on a single verse. Sit and sink into one verse or book. Take your time to eat every word. Savoring the Word is like a wine tasting or a chocolate tasting. Go slow and take your time to enjoy the taste.

Two: Feast in the Word. Read a whole book in one sitting. It's like eating multiple plates at a buffet. Just dive into it. This is for nourishing. Do a bible in a year reading plan. This isn't about quality, but quantity. It isn't a time to study or meditate. This is simply to fill your spirit with the Word. Read large quantities! You don't remember every meal you ate last week, but you know it nourished you. In the same way, doing an aggressive reading plan with large daily quantities isn't for the purpose of savoring, it's just for nourishing.

Three: Read it out loud. The Word is meant to be read out loud. Faith comes by hearing the Word. The greatest declaration you could speak over yourself is the Word of God.

Four: Savor it, feast on it, and read it out loud with others. The Bible is meant for community. Historically in Israel, and in Judaism, the Torah is read publicly daily. They call these times Torah Readings. They chant the word together daily. They have a party every year to celebrate reading the entire book annually. Invite friends to do it with you. Have a get together, fellowship around some snacks, then open the Youversion bible app and read out of the same translation out loud at the same time to snack on the Word.

Activation:

Set aside an hour to do this activation. You can do it alone or with your family and friends.

One: Read Psalm 119 out loud.

Two: Pray in the Spirit for 2 minutes.
Three: Be silent for 4 minutes.
Four: Write down what is highlighted to you.

Bible Facts

The writing of the Bible:

The Bible was written over a 1600 year period by approximately 40 men. The time of the writing was from 1500 BC to AD 100. While the Bible is 1 book, it contain 66 smaller books. The books of the Old Testament were written before the birth of Jesus Christ and the New Testament covers the life of Christ and beyond. While there were at least 40 different people who scribed parts of the Bible, some were more prolific than others. The Apostle Paul scribed at least 13 books of the Bible. He may have also been the scribe of the book of Hebrews. Moses scribed the first 5 books.

The fight to translate the Bible into common language:

1384 AD: John Wycliffe was the first person to produce a (hand- written) manuscript copy of the complete Bible. That was almost 800 years ago. He was declared a heretic because he thought everyone should be allowed to read the Bible in a time when only the church hierarchy had access to it.

1455 AD: Johannes Gutenberg invented the printing press. Books were then able to be produced en-mass instead of individually hand-written. The first book ever printed was Gutenberg's Bible in Latin.

1516 AD: Desiderius Erasmus produced a Greek and Latin New Testament.

1522 AD: Martin Luther released a German New Testament.

1526 AD: William Tyndale released his New Testament, the first New Testament printed in the English Language. He believed every Christian should be able to read their Bible. He was hung and burned at the stake for translating the bible into english.

1611 AD: The King James Bible was released. From John Wycliffe to King James there were over 230 years! It took over 200 years for it to be culturally accepted for the Bible to be available to all believers. Many other Christians were martyred, persecuted and hated for pursuing to make the bible available in common languages. There was such a high price paid to get this bible in our hands.

The Author

Micah Level is the director of Love Pursuit International, a public speaker, and author of many books including the best selling book Words Of Knowledge Training Manual. He has a heart to see the whole body of Christ inspired and empowered to walk out the Great Commission and walk in pure love and devotion to Christ on earth. Signs, wonders, and miracles mark his life, and he is known for his extreme love for God and people. Micah lives in Springfield, Ohio with his wife, Meredith, and their three beautiful children. You can contact him and find more resources at lovepursuitinternational.com

Notes:

Notes:

www.ingramcontent.com/pod-product-compliance
Lightning Source LLC
Chambersburg PA
CBHW051419130726
47989CB00007B/3000